Canine Symphony

Written and Illustrated by Elisa Melville

Copyright © 2024 by Elisa Melville

FIRST EDITION
ISBN: 978-1-7383352-0-6 (Paperback)

Miss Okie gets to play
with her furry friends today

Let's take a look at all the dogs

she'll see

With whippets she will race

With collies she will chase

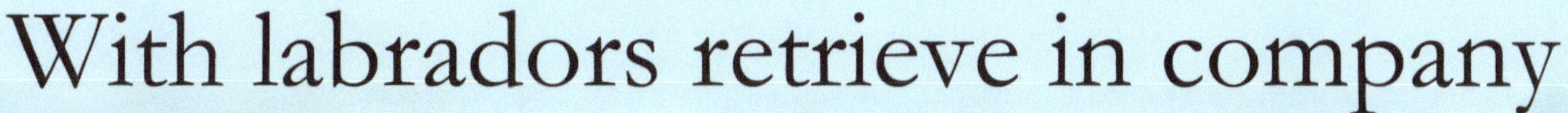

With labradors retrieve in company

With newfies

she will wade

With poodles

she'll parade

And terriers will share the toys

they bring

With great danes
she will bound

With boxers
dig the ground

But with hound dogs she will sing

Ahwoo-oo-oo Ahwoo-oo-oo
They'll howl in perfect harmony

Ahwoo-oo-oo Ahwoo-oo-oo

A kind of canine

symphony

The Bassett

takes the

BASS

The Beagle

sets the pace

The Bloodhound and the Coonhound wail the blues

The Afgan
whips her hair

The Wolfhound
croons with flair

The Dachshund
warbles sweetly to his muse

And Okie though she's shy
will look up to the sky and wag her tail
while others come along

She'll open her mouth wide and
draw a breath inside to bellow out a song!

Ahwoo-oo-oo
Ahwoo-oo-oo
They'll howl in perfect harmony

Ahwoo-oo-oo
Ahwoo-oo-OOOO

A kind of canine symphony

Dog Breed Reference

Which one is your favourite?

Meet the Real "Okie"

I started life as a tiny puppy, but I grew pretty fast!

Now that I'm older, I like to chase my mom and dad on their mountain bikes.

I also like to play with my friends at the dog park!

I enjoy exploring the great outdoors in the sun, rain, or snow.
I especially love to splash in mud puddles and catch snowballs!
When it is nap time, I love to cuddle up with a doggie or human friend.

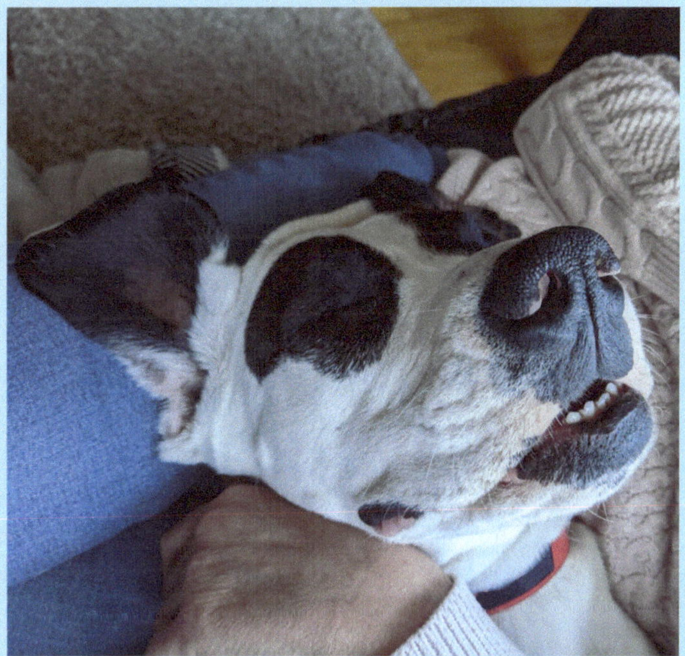

Canine Symphony

Lyrics by Elisa Melville

Composed by Elisa Melville

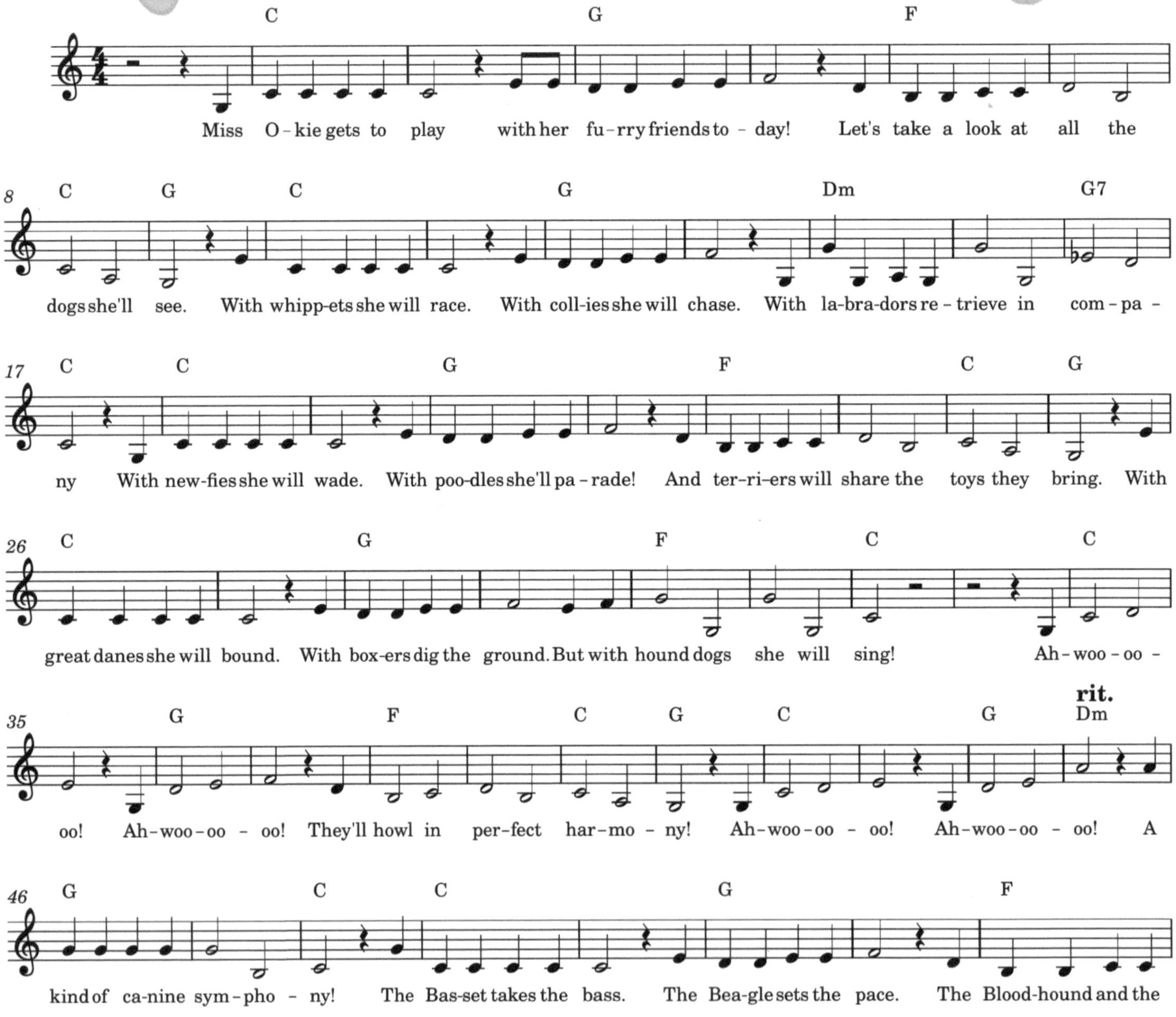

©
Elisa Melville

As mighty Creator,
God formed the brilliant stars,
the lofty mountain peaks,
and the deepest oceans.

As loving Father,
He gave us the humble dog:
a loyal friend who reminds us to laugh
and be grateful for
the simple joys in life.